12 ICONIC AMERICAN MYTHS AND LEGENDS

BLACK RABBIT BOOKS | MARNE VENTURA

Table of Contents

1. John Henry Becomes Famous for Racing a Machine	5
2. Stormy Has Adventures on the High Seas	8
3. Pecos Bill Rides a Tornado in Tall Tales	11
4. Paul Bunyan Grows into a Legendary Giant	14
5. Davy Crockett Reigns over the Frontier	17
6. Johnny Appleseed Sprouts Stories of Kindness	21
7. Annie Oakley Shoots into Stardom	24
8. Betsy Ross' Story Captures America's Fancy	27
9. James Beckwourth Spins Tales about Mountain Life	30
10. Casey Jones Becomes Hero of the Railroad	34
11. Molly Pitcher Represents Women of the Revolution	37
12. Brer Rabbit Overcomes Opponents with Trickery	40
Fact Sheet	44
Glossary	46
For More Information	47
Index	48

John Henry is known for swinging a big hammer to beat a machine.

John Henry Becomes Famous for *Racing a Machine*

John Henry was a fictional African American **folk hero**. He was known as the strongest man on the railroad. Storytellers say he could knock down a mountain with a hammer. Some historians think he was based on a real man.

The real John Henry was born around 1845. He worked for the C&O Railroad. The workers were digging a tunnel through Big Bend Mountain. Henry pounded in steel drills with a hammer. This made holes in the rock. Other workers put explosives in the holes. Then they blasted away the rock. The men chipped away at the mountain for three years. The work was very hard. Hundreds of men died. Henry was known as the strongest man on the job.

Actor Paul Robeson played John Henry in a musical in 1940.

Legend says that Henry could cut through 20 feet (6.1 meters) of rock in 12 hours. One day, a salesman brought a new kind of drill. It was powered by steam. A challenge was set forth—man versus machine. Who could cut through the most rock? Henry swung his big hammer hard and fast. He won! But he died shortly afterward from exhaustion. His story lives on though. He is a **symbol** of strength and determination.

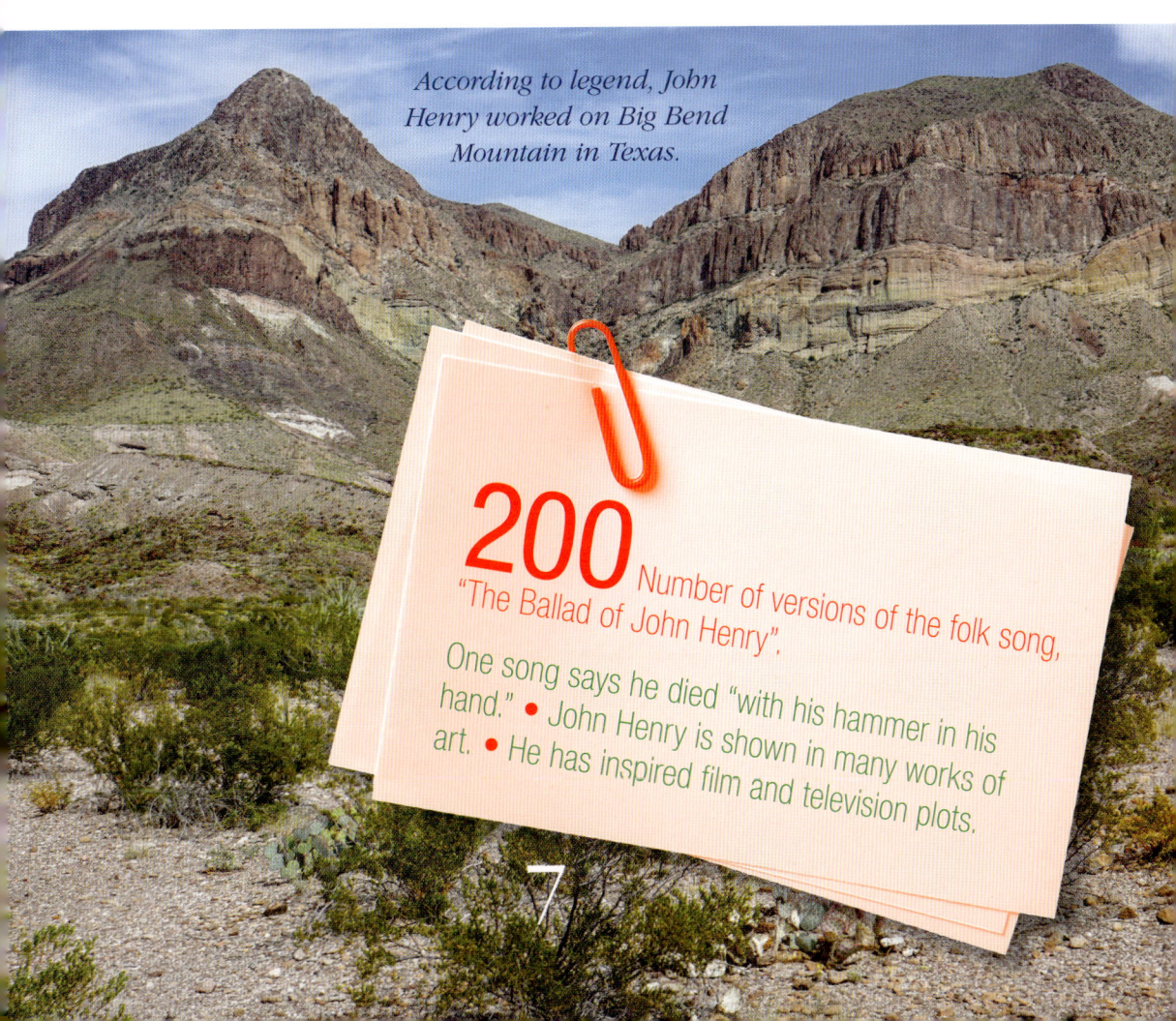

According to legend, John Henry worked on Big Bend Mountain in Texas.

200 Number of versions of the folk song, "The Ballad of John Henry".

One song says he died "with his hammer in his hand." • John Henry is shown in many works of art. • He has inspired film and television plots.

Stormy Has Adventures on the High Seas

2

According to folklore, Alfred Bulltop Stormalong was the best sailor in the world. His nickname was Stormy. He was a giant man. He was born 18 feet (5.5 m) tall and grew taller throughout his life. He worked on his father's ship, *Courser*, starting at age 12. He was the only person strong enough to steer the huge ship. The ship's deck was very long. Sailors had to race on horses from bow to stern to keep watch.

In the 1800s, sailors sang **shanties** about Stormy. In them, Stormy was always brave and bold. Once a huge octopus got caught in the anchor of the ship. Stormy dove into the sea and wrestled the anchor free. Then he tied the legs of the giant octopus into knots.

24 Height in feet (7.3 m) of Captain Stormy, according to legend. The *Courser* was so tall that it needed a hinge in the mast. • The hinge was for folding the mast so it wouldn't hit the Sun or Moon. • The *Courser* was too deep for the Boston Harbor, so it stayed out at sea.

According to legend, Stormy's crew folded the ship's mast down to avoid catching on the Moon.

Stormy was a popular folk hero in the 1800s. Trade by sea was important to Americans during this time. Sailors left New England to buy and sell goods across the Atlantic Ocean. Sailing was a hard, dangerous job. Captain Stormy and the *Courser* symbolize the strength and courage of early American sailors.

Myths A **myth** is an old story that has been told and retold for many years. Some myths express important **values** in the culture that gives rise to them. Some myths are used to explain a practice, belief, or event in nature. Traditionally, myths were not written down.

Stormy was said to sail on a clipper ship, which is designed for speed.

Pecos Bill Rides a Tornado in Tall Tales

Famous cowboy Pecos Bill used a rattlesnake for a lasso. He could ride any horse in Texas. Sometimes he rode a mountain lion. Once he took a ride on a tornado. And it wasn't just any tornado. It was the biggest tornado anyone had ever seen!

Pecos Bill was made up by storytellers. Cowboys told stories about this **frontier** hero. He had **supernatural** skills. The stories are **tall tales**. They were told for fun. In 1917, newsman Edward O'Reilly started writing the stories down. They were printed in a magazine. In O'Reilly's version, Bill's parents were crossing the Pecos River in a wagon. Bill fell out. He was saved and raised by coyotes. Later, he became a cowboy. Other stories say he was so tough that bullets bounced right off his skin. His horse was named Widow-Maker. It ate dynamite.

Drawings of Pecos Bill often show his ridng skills.

Think About It

Why do you think people tell tall tales?

Walt Disney World has a Pecos Bill saloon that people can visit.

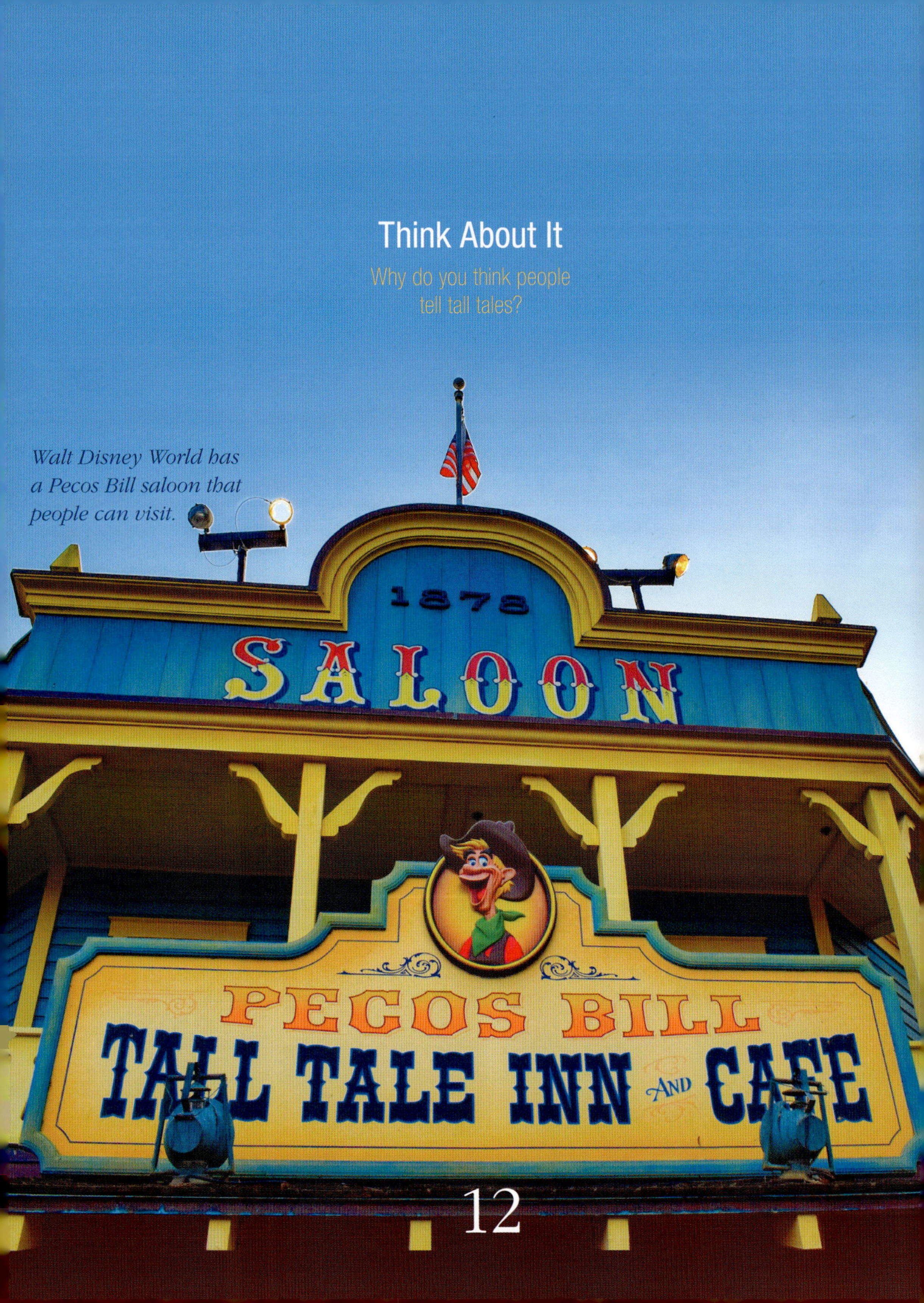

Other writers added to these tales. In one tale, Bill fell in love with Slue-Foot Sue. She was riding a giant fish down a river. He wanted to impress her. He used his rifle to shoot out all the stars in the sky but one. He called it the Lone Star.

While none of the stories are true, people liked retelling them. Pecos Bill became a symbol of the Wild West. He stood for the courage, strength, and humor of cowboys.

9 Years Edward O'Reilly and Jack Warren co-wrote a comic strip about Pecos Bill. The comic strip was written between 1929 and 1938. • O'Reilly published a book, Saga of Pecos Bill, in 1923. • Pecos Bill appeared in a 1948 Disney movie.

Paul Bunyan Grows into a *Legendary Giant*

4

Paul Bunyan was a mythical lumberjack. He crushed whole forests with one swing of his axe. He dug the Great Lakes. His booming voice made tree branches fall.

Loggers started telling tall tales about Paul Bunyan in the 1880s. In early stories, the hero was big and strong. He stood 7 feet (2.1 m) tall. Around 1910, the stories were being published. Logging companies also ran ads starring the giant. That's how many Americans learned the stories.

Paul Bunyan became a national folk hero. Stories about him became more fantastic. He was so big he used a pine tree as a comb. His heavy footprints formed lakes. He had a giant blue ox named Babe. The ox was strong too. Over the years, Paul Bunyan and Babe have appeared in songs, art, and children's

Lumberjacks used to use axes to chop down trees.

14

15

stories. Even poets, such as Robert Frost and Carl Sandberg, wrote about him.

Historians don't know if Paul Bunyan was inspired by a real man. It's more likely he represents hard work and persistence. These were the traits valued by loggers. Paul Bunyan is a symbol of strength and energy.

There are many statues of Paul Bunyan and Babe, like this one in Klamath, California.

1,000 About the number of books that have mentioned Paul Bunyan.

Storytellers say Paul Bunyan made the Grand Canyon. • They say his camp stove was so big it covered an acre (0.4 hectare) of land. • Bunyan was popular among loggers in the Midwest.

Davy Crockett Reigns over *the Frontier*

Davy Crockett was known as the King of the Wild West. Storytellers said he could leap over the Ohio River. He could carry a steamboat on his back. He appeared in books and plays starting in the 1800s. Crockett battled wildcats with his bare hands. He killed bears with a single shot. In the 1950s, his stories were shown on television and in films. His image was put on shoes, shirts, and lunch boxes.

The legend was loosely based on a real person. The real David Crockett did not fight snakes or alligators. He was born in 1786. He grew up in Tennessee. He served as a military **scout** before entering politics. Crockett was elected to the Tennessee government in 1821. He also served in the US House of

Representatives. A colleague called him the "gentleman from the cane." This referred to the wilderness where Crockett hunted. Crockett had a rugged look. People began telling wild stories about him.

Crockett moved to Texas in 1835. There, his fame grew. He helped the Texans fight for independence from Mexico. Crockett was killed in 1836 at the Battle of the Alamo.

Crockett represented the traits needed by American settlers moving west. He was brave, hard-working, and persistent.

7 million Number of copies sold in six months of the 1955 song "The Ballad of Davy Crockett".

Davy Crockett was born into poverty. • He had only 100 days of schooling. • He fought for better treatment of American Indians.

COONSKIN CAPS In the 1950s, the TV show, *Davy Crockett*, set off a trend. In the show, Crockett wears a coonskin cap. It is made of raccoon fur. Soon, millions of kids began wearing the caps. They wanted to look like Crockett's character. At the show's peak, 5,000 caps were sold per day in the United States.

Johnny Appleseed Sprouts Stories *of Kindness*

Johnny Appleseed was a new type of frontier hero. His fame was not for strength or courage. He carried seeds instead of a weapon. He planted apple trees across America.

Johnny Appleseed was actually John Chapman. He lived from 1774 to 1845. Tales paint him as a wanderer. He planted seeds wherever he went. But Chapman was a businessman. He grew seedlings. He sold them for profit. He sold thousands of seedlings to **pioneers**. They planted apple orchards. They used the apples as a food source. They made cider too.

Over the years, Appleseed was featured in many songs, plays, and tales. In one story, he built a fire in a log. To his surprise, he found bear cubs inside it. He put the fire out and slept in the cold.

These stories were based on Chapman's **reputation**. He was known for being cheerful and generous. He was gentle with animals. He made money from his business. But sometimes he met families without much money. He gave them seedlings for free. Johnny Appleseed stories honor Chapman for his kindness and generosity. He helped pioneers start farms and settle the West.

Think About It
Johnny Appleseed is kind and generous. Other legends have strong or hard-working characters. What traits do you think a hero should have?

Johnny Appleseed traveled a lot to help other people.

1,200 About the number of planted acres (486 ha) owned by John Chapman.

- Johnny Appleseed was portrayed in a Disney movie in 1948.
- He helped prepare the way for 19th-century pioneers.
- Settlers in the Midwest used the apple orchards he planted to make a living.

Chapman helped plant apple orchards in many US states and some places in Canada.

Annie Oakley Shoots into *Stardom*

7 Annie Oakley was a real person. Unlike some folktale characters, many of her deeds were true. She was a sharpshooter. With her rifle, Oakley could shoot a playing card from 30 paces away. She could shoot a dime tossed up into the air. Oakley was the star of Buffalo Bill's Wild West show.

Oakley was born in 1860 in Ohio. Her real name was Phoebe Ann Mosey. She taught herself to fire a gun at a young age. Mosey hunted quail for her family. At age 15, Mosey won a shooting contest. She won against a famous marksman. People were impressed. She started traveling with performance groups. She used the stage name Annie Oakley. In 1885, she joined Buffalo Bill's show and traveled the world.

Annie Oakley's fame continued in films and plays. These are loosely based on her life. There is a 1946

Annie Oakley won many awards for her impressive shooting skills.

5 *Height in feet (1.5 m) of Annie Oakley.*

She was the first female to be famous as a sharpshooter. • She was very thrifty with the money she earned. • She gave money to orphan charities and her family.

musical called *Annie Get Your Gun*. Some songs from this are still big hits. People are drawn to her story. At a time when most sharpshooters were men, she was a trailblazer for women.

Actress Ethel Merman (left) played Annie Oakley in the Broadway musical.

BUFFALO BILL Buffalo Bill's real name was William Cody. He was a buffalo hunter, army scout, soldier, and performer. In 1883, he started a Wild West show. It featured sharpshooters and trick riders. It had live animals such as buffalo and bears. It ran for 30 years. The show performed all over the world.

Betsy Ross' Story Captures *America's Fancy*

Betsy Ross was a seamstress in Philadelphia. Her husband died in the American Revolution. After his death, she took over the family's business. She covered furniture with cloth and leather.

Legend has it that Ross sewed the first American flag. George Washington visited her home in 1776. He asked her to sew a flag for the new nation. He showed her a rough design. Ross suggested using stars with five points instead of six. Washington used her ideas to make a new sketch. Then Ross stitched the first flag in her back parlor.

Ross' grandson, William J. Canby, first told this story in 1870. Canby said this story was passed down through his family. But no proof has been found. Historians do not think it is a true story. Still, Americans have been telling it for more than 100 years. Many like the idea. They think of

STAR-SPANGLED BANNER

Another famous seamstress is Mary Pickersgill. She made the Star-Spangled Banner. It flew over Fort McHenry during the War of 1812. It inspired the national **anthem**.

13 Number of stars and stripes on the first American flag.

Betsy Ross was born Elizabeth Griscom in 1752. She died in 1836. • The Continental Congress adopted the flag in 1777. • Although historians can't prove she made the first flag, Ross is an American icon.

Ross as a bold widow who ran her own business. They enjoy the thought of Washington himself making the request. The story has come to stand for patriotism and public service.

In 1893, Charles Weisberger painted a picture of Betsy Ross. In it, Ross is showing the flag to Washington. The painting became very popular. It drew more attention to the legend.

In a painting, Betsy Ross shows Major Ross and Robert Morris (middle) how she cut the stars for the first US flag.

James Beckwourth Spins Tales about *Mountain Life*

9

James Beckwourth was born in the late 1700s. His mother was an enslaved black woman, and his father was her white slaveholder. This meant he was born enslaved. Beckwourth's father freed him as an adult. Beckwourth moved west. He became a fur trapper in the Rocky Mountains. He survived in the wild. He also lived among the Crow American Indians for six years. In about 1850, Beckwourth discovered a new passage through the Sierra Nevada Mountains.

Beckwourth often told stories around campfires. Most of these stories were about himself. He was known to **exaggerate** his strength and skills. Beckwourth told his stories to a traveling newsman named Thomas Bonner. Bonner wrote a book to tell Beckwourth's stories. It was

30

Some of Beckwourth's stories were about his own hunting and shooting skills.

published in 1856. Soon many people were enjoying the stories. Beckwourth created his own legends about his life.

Beckwourth stands out as a unique black pioneer. People of many races explored the American West. But Beckwourth was the only one to share his adventures. He helped settle the West. He is a symbol of Black Americans who left their mark on history.

5,221 Elevation in feet (1,591 m) of Beckwourth Pass.

James Beckwourth lived from 1798 to 1867. • In 1823, he was hired to tend horses for fur traders. • He served in the Mexican War and Cheyenne War of 1864.

MOUNTAIN MEN Pioneers who trapped fur in the Rocky Mountains were called mountain men. They trapped beavers in streams. They sold the fur for profit. Some men like Beckwourth spent a lot of time with American Indians. Sometimes the trappers adopted their way of life and beliefs.

Beckwourth (right) was accepted by the Crow tribe.

Casey Jones Becomes Hero of the Railroad

10

Casey Jones was always on time. He was a train engineer. Folks set their clocks by his train, "Cannonball." Casey's real name was Jonathan Luther Jones. People called him Casey after his hometown, Cayce, Kentucky.

On April 30, 1900, a train car was stuck on the track. "Cannonball" was speeding too fast to stop in time. Jones knew it would crash. He blew the train whistle to warn the passengers. He hit the brakes as hard as he could to slow the train. He yelled at his assistant, Sim Webb, to jump from the train. Webb survived. Jones did not. But his heroic actions saved everyone else on board.

Wallace Saunders was a friend of Jones. He wrote a song after Jones' death, "The **Ballad** of Casey Jones."

Throughout his time working with trains, Jones was often considered to be a risk taker.

1 million

About the number of copies sold of "The Ballad of Casey Jones" by 1914.

- Jones worked on the Illinois Central Railroad.
- Tales of his bravery show up in French, German, and Afrikaans songs.
- His image was on a US stamp in 1950.

It told the heroic story of the day he died. Railroad workers began to sing it along Jones' old railroad line. One of them passed it along to professional songwriters. Soon different versions were performed on stage or recorded. It became a traditional folk song. Johnny Cash and the Grateful Dead even sang about him. Jones is an American icon. He embodies bravery and selflessness.

Johnny Cash

MOLLY PITCHER
Represents Women
of the Revolution

Many female colonists helped fight during the American Revolution. They worked at the army camps. They kept the tents clean. They cooked food. According to legend, Molly Pitcher was one such woman. The tale takes place during the Battle of Monmouth in 1778. Molly carried pitchers of water to soldiers manning the cannons, hence her nickname. When her husband was wounded, she took over his cannon. She fired it for the rest of the battle.

Some historians think Molly Pitcher was actually Mary Hays McCauly. Military records show McCauly's husband fought in the Revolution. The state of Pennsylvania paid her for some sort of military service. Records do not say what she actually did. Margaret Corbin also has been identified as Molly Pitcher. Corbin fought at the Battle of Fort Washington in 1776. Records show the military considered her a soldier.

Others think that Molly Pitcher was not one person. Rather, she represented all women who helped during the American Revolution. Since the 1850s, songs, art, books, and films have told Molly Pitcher's tale. She is an iconic heroine of America's fight for independence.

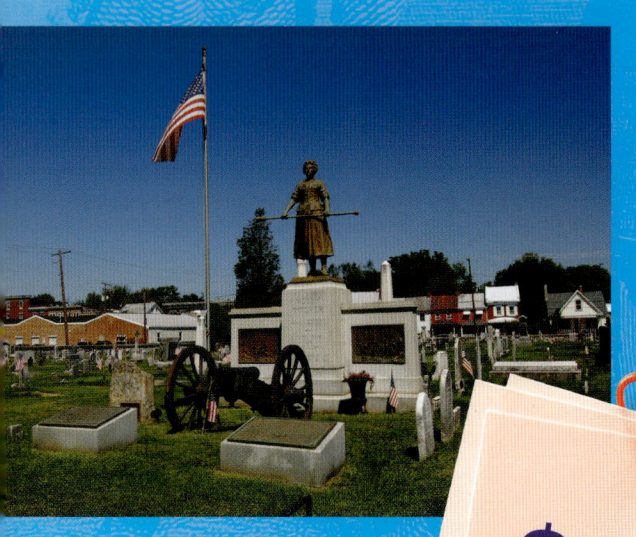

Molly Pitcher's grave in Carlisle, Pennsylvania, honors her service to her country.

$40 Amount Mary Hays McCauly was paid per year for her services in the war.

Women played an important role in winning the Revolutionary War. • Women who traveled with the army were known as camp followers. • Sometimes women disguised themselves as men in order to fight.

Many soldiers were surprised by Pitcher's courage in battle.

39

Brer Rabbit
Overcomes Opponents
with Trickery

12

Brer Rabbit was a popular character in African-American tales. He was good at outsmarting other animals. In one story, Brer Rabbit is caught in a trap. He tricks Brer Fox into taking his place. In another, the rabbit falls down a well. He tricks the fox into saving him. These trickster tales were often very funny. Brer Rabbit was a symbol of cleverness.

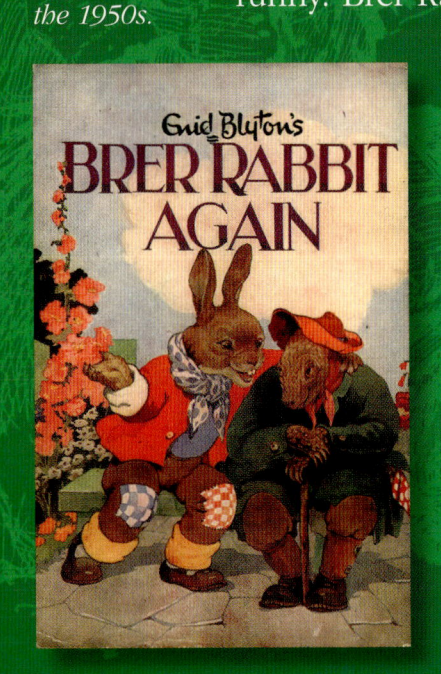

Brer Rabbit was published in the UK in the 1950s.

Brer Rabbit stories were first told in Africa. Africans who were enslaved by Americans continued to tell the stories. The storytellers used places or experiences from their daily lives. The stories spoke about inequality. Enslaved people had very little freedom. They lived in harsh conditions. Most were not allowed to learn to read or write.

Think About It Oral storytelling is an important part of many cultures. Why do you think this is? What can stories tell us about a culture?

They could be punished for complaining about their lives. The animal characters often stood for the storytellers. They shared the smart ways they learned to survive.

Joel Chandler Harris was a journalist. He had heard Brer Rabbit tales as a child. In 1879, he began recording them. Harris published the tales in books beginning in 1881. Now, Brer Rabbit has fans around the world. Stories have been printed in more than 30 languages. Brer Rabbit represents the idea that a weaker person can overcome a stronger enemy through wit.

1881 Year when Joel Chandler Harris' first Brer Rabbit book was published. Uncle Remus is the narrator of Brer Rabbit stories. Harris used African, European, and Native American folklore in his stories. The stories have influenced famous writers such as Mark Twain.

The books include illustrations of the Brer sharing stories with younger rabbits.

Fact

- Several organizations exist to study and preserve cultural folklore. The American Folklore Society was founded in 1888. Members study folklore from around the world. The American Folklife Center was created in 1976 as part of the Library of Congress. Its purpose is to research, preserve, and educate people about American folklore.

- Songs are popular ways to tell and retell myths and legends. Many of the stories in this book have songs connected to them. The Library of Congress has the largest collection of folk songs in the United States.

- Some American legends feature patriotic heroes, such as Betsy Ross or Molly Pitcher. These stories express popular American values, such as honesty or service.

Betsy Ross

Molly Pitcher

George Washington

Sheet

- Many stories have been told about George Washington to portray him as a hero. According to one made-up story, Washington cut down a cherry tree. When his father asked him about it, he admitted to cutting it down. "I cannot tell a lie," he said.

- Disney has produced several short films on American legends. *The Legend of Johnny Appleseed* came out in 1948. In 1950, *The Brave Engineer* told the story of Casey Jones. The short movie *Paul Bunyan* was released in 1958. *John Henry* came out in 2000.

Paul Bunyan

Johnny Appleseed

John Henry

Casey Jones

Glossary

anthem
A formal song of loyalty, praise, or happiness.

ballad
A kind of poem or song that tells a story.

exaggerate
To describe something as larger or greater than it really is.

folk hero
A person who is greatly admired by many people of a particular place.

frontier
A distant area where few people live.

legend
A story based on a real person or events.

myth
A story told to explain a practice, belief, or natural occurrance.

pioneer
Someone who is one of the first people to live in a new area.

reputation
The overall quality or character as judged by people in general.

scout
A member of a military unit who goes ahead to gather information.

shanty
A song that sailors sang in the past while they worked.

supernatural
Unable to be explained by science or the laws of nature.

symbol
An object or action that expresses or represents an idea or quality.

tall tale
A story that is very difficult to believe.

values
A principle or quality that is valuable or desirable.

For More Information

Books

Bell, Samantha. *Johnny Appleseed: The Making of a Myth.* Ann Arbor, MI: Cherry Lake Publishing, 2024.

Furstinger, Nancy. *Davy Crockett.* New York: AV2 by Weigl, 2020.

Lombardo, Jennifer. *A Guide to Native American Myths.* Buffalo, NY: Cavendish Square Publishing, 2025.

Websites

American Folklore: Myths and Legends
www.americanfolklore.net/category/myths-legends/

Myths, Folktales & Fairy Tales
teacher.scholastic.com/writewit/mff/index.htm

About the Author

Marne Ventura is a children's book author and a former elementary school teacher. She holds a master's degree in education with an emphasis in reading and language development from the University of California.

Index

American Indians, 18, 32, 33
Appleseed, Johnny, 21, 22, 23, 45

Babe, 14
Beckwourth, James, 30, 31, 32, 33
Bill, Buffalo, 24, 26
Bill, Pecos, 11, 12, 13
books, 13, 16, 17, 30, 38, 40, 42
Bunyan, Paul, 14, 15, 16, 45

Chapman, John, 21, 22, 23
Crockett, Davy, 17, 18, 19, 20

Henry, John, 4, 5, 6, 7, 45

Jones, Casey, 34, 35, 36, 45

movies, 13, 23, 45
musicals, 6, 26

Oakley, Annie, 24, 25, 26

Pitcher, Molly, 37, 38, 39, 44

Rabbit, Brer, 40, 41, 42, 43
Ross, Betsy, 27, 28, 29, 44

songs, 7, 14, 18, 21, 26, 34, 35, 36, 38, 44
Star-Spangled Banner, The, 28
Stormy, 8, 9, 10

TV series, 7, 17

wars, 28, 32, 38
Wild West, 13, 17, 24, 26

Copyright © 2025 Black Rabbit Books. All rights reserved. No part of this book may be reproduced in any form without written permission from the publisher. • Top Rank is an imprint of Black Rabbit Books. • Edited by Alissa Thielges | Designed by Danny Nanos • Photographs © Alamy Stock Photo/Old Paper Studios, 40, Pictures Now, 22, 45, Retro AdArchives, 40, The History Collection, 35, 45; Associated Press, 26; Dreamstime/Brenda Kean, 36, Calvin L. Leake, 24, Chiyacat, 20, Curtis Heideman, cover, 1, Jeffreymetcalf31, 18–19, Larry Metayer, 4–5, Michael Flippo, 27, Nico99, 11, Sean Pavone, 12–13, Sumi Akther, 23, Vivaltours, 12; Getty Images/Bettmann, 42, 43, Universal History Archive, 36; Library of Congress/Currier & Ives, 10, Detroit Publishing Co., 2-3, 14–15, Ferris, Jean Leon Gerome, 29, 44, Fox, R. K. (Richard Kyle), 25; Pexels/Pixabey, 34; Public Domain/ 6, 45, Arthur Burdett "A.B." Frost, 41; Shutterstock/Belinda Pretorius, 48; Christos Georghiou, 10, Dan Thornberg, 28, Daniel M. Silva, 38, Eric Isselee, 20, Everett Collection, 31, f11photo, 17, George Sheldon, 37, Gerry Matthews, 16, JMY Photography, 7, Jolygon, 46-47, Krasowit, 8–9, La fotisto, 14, Marianoblanco, 44, Mashikomo, 32, neftali, 30, Perry Correll, 28, Pinkcandy, 2, 15, 45, Ron and Joe, 5, roundex, 4, Tim UR, 21, Tony Baggett, 26; Wikimedia Commons/Harris & Ewing, 28, public domain, 33, 38-39, 44, 21 • Printed in China

Library of Congress Cataloging-in-Publication Data Names: Ventura, Marne, author. | Title: 12 iconic American myths and legends / By Marne Ventura. | Description: Mankato, MN: Black Rabbit Books, [2025] | Series: Iconic America | Includes bibliographical references and index. | Audience: Ages 9–13 | Grades 4–6 | Identifiers: LCCN 2024020323 | ISBN 9781645823964 (library binding) | ISBN 9781645824183 (paperback) | ISBN 9781645824404 (ebook) | Subjects: LCSH: Legends—United States—Juvenile literature. | Folklore—United States—Juvenile literature. | Tales—United States—Juvenile literature. | United States—History—Juvenile literature. | Classification: LCC GR105 .V46 2025 | DDC 398.20973—dc23/ eng/20240514 | LC record available at https://lccn.loc.gov/2024020323